SPIRIT

Deansgate, an arrow-straight thoroughfare from the Beetham Tower to the cathedral, is a natural processional route, usually choked with stationary traffic. But there are ephemeral events which lift the spirit of those who take the time explore various diversions along the way. Extensions to the Rylands Library provide a modern foil to its Victorian splendour. The People's History Museum is going through a similar transition in the Pump House. New development continues to create urban spaces amongst legal offices and, on cold winter days, ice-skating brings relief from more serious business. In the commercial centre, the tranquility of the Barton Arcade leads to the humane bustle of St Ann's Square with its buskers, continental food and craft markets and the truly spiritual experience of the Royal Exchange Theatre.

Towers
of glass rise up
from Deansgate to Arndale.
The vibrant joys of the city
beckon.

The Beetham Tower, rising above the ever-present traffic, marks the southern end of Deansgate as it progresses through legal, commercial and retail areas, with links to cultural gems along the way.

She sits,
in icy winds,
watching, waiting, wishing
she had a horse, a kingdom, a
warm coat.

*A worthwhile diversion down narrow side streets
can often reveal surprises which could go
unnoticed, like the surreal mannequin sitting on
the parapet of "The Old Nag's Head"
in Lloyd Street.*

Modern
structures highlight
Gothic decoration;
dark internal spaces cloister
knowledge.

Extensions at the John Rylands Library are an effective foil to the original building by Basil Champneys (1890-9), commissioned by Enriqueta as a lasting memorial to her husband.

Crafted
words rise and fall;
echoes tangle the sounds
with alien noise from passing
traffic.

Students from Manchester University read their work to an audience in the Historic Entrance Hall of the John Rylands Library to mark the exhibition " A Small Eternity: The Shape of the Sonnet Through Time".

New Year
lawyers have left
an empty quarter to
ice-skaters in the shadow of
Justice.

Over the Christmas and New Year holiday period, a temporary ice-skating rink was installed in Hardman Square, adjacent to the Manchester Civil Justice Centre with its remarkable cantilevered structure and exciting colour scheme.

Trends in
working class food
express identity;
cross the river to Mark Addy
for lunch.

*The People's History Museum examined changes in
food in the exhibition "From Butties to Bhajis".
Pub lunches are legendary at the "Mark Addy"
across the Irwell. It is named after a Victorian
publican renowned and honoured for rescuing
drowning people from the river.*

Skewered
to Salford's bank,
the main span hangs in space
from a cat's cradle of threads, tied
to earth.

Trinity Bridge over the River Irwell was designed
by Santiago Calatrava (1993-5), providing a link for
new development around the Lowry Hotel, leaving
the occasional glimpse of the cathedral.

Lunchtime
escapists, from
hard-hatted builders to
hard-headed bankers, seek tastes of
the Med.

*Katsouris Café and Deli on Deansgate, an offshoot
from their original establishment at Bury Market,
brings individuality and quality to fast food.*

Urbane
Renaissance grace
in cast iron and glass
gives respite from bustling crowds and
traffic.

Barton Arcade, built in 1871, is home to specialist shops and cafes exploiting the ambience of its distinctive interior, influenced by the Galleria Vittorio Emanuele in Milan.

Subtle
spiced aromas
entice hungry people
to paella bubbling in a
vast pan.

Regular food festivals, craft markets and other
events bring life to St Ann's Square with fast food
stalls to supplement the permanent food outlets
which spill out into the square in good weather.

Elvis?
No, a busker
strumming with taped backing;
a coin dropped into guitar case earns
a smile.

Outdoor performers are another regular feature of St Ann's Square throughout the year, and they brighten the day no matter what the weather does to dampen spirits.

A host
of umbrellas
gather to join in a
celebration of jazz, blues and
gospel.

*The closing concert in St Ann's Square for the
Manchester Jazz Festival 2009 defied the weather
as Paul Bentley and the Jazz Prescription
presented a selection of the music of Ray Charles.*

Echoes
from "noises off"
give extra dimensions
to battles raging around the
Great Hall.

The timeless nature of Shakespeare's work demonstrates, in a cold grey stage set, the futility of war and the responsibility of leadership in the Royal Exchange production of "Henry V".

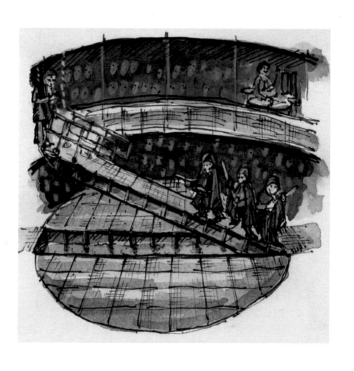

Exposed
to high culture
in a Norfolk cottage,
a family waits for a man
in vain.

*The wildness of the Norfolk landscape recreated in
the Royal Exchange Theatre for Arnold Wesker's
"Roots" contrasts with the homecoming of a young
woman who has seen life in London.*

Amidst
smells of cabbage,
a fugitive son sees
his risen father die - and rise
again.

The condition of ordinary people who wrestle with the political and cultural problems of Ireland is explored in the atmospheric presentation of J M Synge's "Playboy of the Western World" in the Royal Exchange Theatre.

*A salutary rainbow arches over Gorton Priory
designed by Pugin as the Monastery of St Francis
(1866-72).*